Grandpa Dean

from: MN.

**This book is dedicated
to the friends of the circus and the
unique world of variety entertainment**

ISBN: 1480260800
ISBN-13: 978-1480260801

"You Like It? I Do It Again."

The Dieter Tasso Story
as told to Ron Dentinger

Dieter Tasso

Acknowledgements

A special "Thank You" to:

Tom Diehl, Irene Fosset, John Buecheler, Evi Kelly, Heinz Pichler, Syliva Pichler, Rich Renik , Bernice Kurzynski, Theresa Donnelly and Janice Hartwig.

Foreword | Tom Diehl

I remember the first time I met Dieter Tasso. It was 1977. Tommy Bartlett and I were in the audience at the Hacienda Casino in Las Vegas, searching for stage acts for *The Tommy Bartlett Ski, Sky, and Stage Show* in Wisconsin Dells, Wisconsin. Dieter was among the vaudeville-type acts in the Hacienda's production show. We, and everyone else in the audience, were entertained by Dieter's showmanship and skill, performing his signature cup-and-saucer act on a slack wire. Tommy and I knew that Dieter would be a popular addition to our show, so we signed him for the 1978 season.

Chicago-area radio personality and master showman Tommy Bartlett started the *Tommy Bartlett Show* on the shores of Lake Delton, in Wisconsin Dells, in 1953. The show was and continues to be known for its high-quality, family oriented entertainment on water, on stage, and high in the sky.

Fast-forward sixty years: The *Tommy Bartlett Show* is one of the last venues to incorporate vaudeville acts into a water-ski and stage-show format, and Dieter Tasso is still entertaining our audiences today. Dieter's act has changed over the years from a strictly physical juggling performance to a combination juggling/comedy act. Dieter learned to utilize his juggling to become a great comedian, which suits our audiences well, as laughter is an important ingredient in the *Tommy Bartlett Show*.

While Dieter has that rare ability to make us laugh, over the years I've also learned that Dieter is a loyal friend. On June 9, 2008, after torrential rains caused Lake Delton to break through its banks and drain into the Wisconsin River, I had 120 people relying on us for summer jobs, but no lake on which to present a ski show. I needed to quickly reconfigure the show, adding extra stage talent, so that we could keep it going and fulfill our commitment to our employees and visitors.

The first call I made was to Dieter who had chosen to retire when his wife, Irene, became ill, but it didn't even take him two seconds to say yes to me. Within four days, Dieter and Irene were in Wisconsin Dells and Dieter was performing on our stage once again. For someone who had planned to retire, Dieter ended up working the rest of the summer, just as good as ever.

After Irene passed away in 2010, Dieter called me, asking if I would have room for him to perform that summer. I told him that we would always have room for him, and he once again made the trek to the Dells where he was embraced by his Tommy Bartlett family and friends.

I've known Dieter Tasso for thirty-six years. I respect him for being a gifted comedian and talented performer, but I respect him even more for his outstanding character and for being a genuine and loyal friend.

Tom Diehl

Tom Diehl joined the Tommy Bartlett organization in 1967 as manager of Housing and Food Operations. He was promoted to general manager in 1973, and in 1981 he was named president of Tommy Bartlett, Inc.

With the passing of Tommy Bartlett in 1998, Tom and his wife, Margaret, became co-owners of Tommy Bartlett, Inc.

Preface

There not only is a place for humor in our daily lives, there is a need for humor in our daily lives. Without going into a lot of detail I will point out that laughter is mentally and physically healthy. It's one of the times that the brain releases endorphins, which can induce a natural euphoria.

Science can explain why we laugh, and science can explain why laughing is healthy, but you will notice that, while science can explain why we laugh and why laughing is healthy, very few scientists excel at making people laugh.

Laughter is an incredibly unique force for good. You can't laugh with someone and hate the person at the same time. I'm often quoted with my line:

> Laughter unites people. There is an attitude adjustment that takes place when you laugh. In fact, I seriously recommend that someone should plant a few whoopee cushions in the United Nations.

Science can describe the process, and science can also prescribe the treatment, but if the prescription is "laughter," science is unable to provide that proverbial best medicine.

People also love to be amazed, whether it's by a musician, a magician, or in this case, a juggler. Being in awe of something is stimulating all by itself, but occasionally we also experience that unique magical combination of laughter and amazement—at the same time. During these times you can momentarily let your problems go while your endorphins flow.

I can't remember when I wasn't interested in humor. It was my love of laughter that led to my Humor Library. The library fills a room and has to be the largest library of its kind, anywhere. It includes over a thousand books, magazines, videos, and audio selections spanning over 250 years of the evolution of humor and entertainment. The library contains books about why people laugh, how to make people laugh, and how to write jokes. It includes hundreds of joke books by category with sections on humorous quotes, humorous poetry and limericks, and practical jokes. But one section of the library, Medicine Shows, Side Shows, Vaudeville, and the Circus, is the section of the library that inspired my interest in variety entertainment.

Dieter Tasso's juggling skills, combined with his ongoing hilarious patter, had me totally impressed. It rekindled my already considerable interest in variety entertainment. I had heard that Dieter had a very interesting life and I wondered if I could find his biography documented in a book for my library. I looked. There was no book, so I decided to write one.

Ron Dentinger

Contents

Introduction

In this book, Ron Dentinger brings us in close contact with the life behind the limelight of the great circus and entertainment world. It is an insight into the personality of performing artist Dieter Tasso: the man, the ideals, and the emotions that moved him; some of the nine lives in a struggle for survival; and most of all, his generous contribution in bringing joy to humankind and making people laugh. May the story of his life also be an encouragement to young artists to strive toward the best they can be.

Starting with antique historic records of juggling, we are transported to Dieter's incarnation. Although his birth was not announced by a comet, he was a most desired child. He was the second-last to be born. Unfortunately, in a world of turmoil, his parents each met untimely recalls from this world. Eventually, his uncle and aunt took him under their wings in Berlin. The story evolves from the early Berlin days, coming to the US, and *The Greatest Show On Earth*, to Las Vegas, to cruise ships, and traveling the world, to the numerous television shows, and the many years at the Crazy Horse Saloon in Paris, the Wintergarten in Berlin, and the Apollo in Duesseldorf, to thirty-five years at the *Tommy Bartlett Show*, and the GOP Variety in Hanover, and many more.

Throughout his life, we see that the thing that makes Dieter genuinely happy is when he can bring the souls of his audience together in a moment of joy and happiness. It is the reason he was honored with a permanent plaque in bronze, embedded at Sarasota's St. Armands Circle, where artists are recorded for posterity. However, Dieter is not thinking of posterity. Right now heaven can wait. Far from retiring, he is approaching eighty as he buoyantly continues performing on the international scene. May he live to be one hundred and twenty.

John Buecheler, a Friend of Show Folks

Timeline #1, 1994 AD: Prologue

I first met Dieter Tasso when I was brought in to fill one of the entertainment slots at the *Tommy Bartlett Show*. I was contacted by Tom Diehl to fill in for the scheduled act that for some reason could not take the stage. I am a comic/humorist. I travel the US and Canada on the banquet circuit, and now and then I am also hired as "The Opening Act" for various nationally known entertainers.

In the United States, thanks largely to television, variety acts are an entertainment form that is seldom seen anymore. Variety entertainment started long before vaudeville and it went strong into the 1970s, but today variety entertainment is rare, especially as seen as a live stage show like that provided by the acts at the *Tommy Bartlett Show*. Dieter Tasso's unique routine in particular really caught my interest. The talent was impressive and the likeability of the man was infectious. In a very real way this was a trip into the past, and that's where I'd like to start, in the past.

The year is 1994, and it is another fun-filled summer night at the Wisconsin Dells. On stage at the *Tommy Bartlett Show* is comedy juggler, Dieter Tasso, working to a full house. At one point he stops. The laughter also stops, and Dieter says, "I want to attempt something difficult. The last time this particular feat was successfully performed was by the great Enrico Rastelli, shortly before he died." Dieter pauses and then adds, "And I don't feel so good tonight either." And the laughter rolls once again. And that's typical Tasso. But I'm getting way ahead of myself. Let me go back to the beginning. And I mean, "The very beginning."

1

Timeline #2, 1994 BC: The Beginning

We need to time-travel backward about four thousand years, from 1994 AD, back to 1994 BC. This is the beginning. A Wikipedia article, "The History of Juggling," tells about an ancient Egyptian wall painting that appears to depict "toss jugglers." The picture on the wall is from the fifteenth Beni Hassan tomb of an unknown prince, and it depicts four female dancers and acrobats throwing balls. It is the earliest known record of toss juggling.

The evolution then proceeds to: China, Greece, the Roman Empire, and Europe. It seems that in Europe, between 500 AD and 1500 AD, jugglers would perform in the marketplaces, on the streets, at fairs, and in drinking houses. They would perform short, humorous, and often bawdy acts, and then they would pass a hat or bag among the audience for tips.

Some of the pictures in this book are a lower resolution than the publisher recommends. They may be dark and/or faded. They are included because they help tell the story.

Timeline #3, 1934 AD: Fast-forward to 1934 AD, Berlin, Germany

Dieter Krakow was born in Berlin, Germany, on Monday, January 8, 1934. He may have been predestined to be a juggler because his mother and father, his brother, and two of his uncles were all jugglers. His parents were a juggling duo known as "The Krakows," but their career was winding down by the time Dieter was born.

Dieter remembers those war years. His early days were tough, and in my first interview with him he talked about those early days:

When I was born, there was no hospital involved. My mother had me at home with the help of a midwife. I had two older brothers, one older sister, and one younger sister. We lived in the middle of Berlin, in an apartment. The apartment was four flights up, with no elevator. My earliest memories go back to when I was about five or six years old. I remember my parents sent me to a school that was about two blocks away.

We stayed in Berlin until about 1942, and then my father moved the family to Karow, a little town that's just north of Berlin. We lived there in half of a house. The other half belonged to somebody else. They cut it right in half. They even painted the front of the house two different colors. With the exception of one cold-water spigot in the kitchen, the house wasn't equipped with any plumbing. This was a huge problem because Mother Nature equipped me with plumbing, but the new house was on a piece of land that had enough room for a garden. My father always wanted a garden. The garden had a plum tree and an apple tree and lots of bushes. My father really enjoyed trying to be a farmer.

The war raged on, and at night, in the distance, we could see Berlin burning from our home in Karow. My father wanted his kids farther away from Berlin and farther away from the bombing. He sent me away to military school in Bavaria, which was in the south of Germany, well away from Berlin. I was eight or nine years old.

For what it's worth, military school in the Third Reich wasn't what people probably think. There wasn't very much political stuff taught in military school. We were probably too young for that, but we did have schooling, for which I am happy because I missed a lot of schooling due to the war. The little bit of education that I got along the way, I got at the military school.

In about 1944, they drafted my father. They didn't draft him earlier because he worked for the post office, and the military thought that was an important job; plus he had five kids, so he entered the military late. Then I remember the day he came home for a vacation, and he overstayed. Every soldier had a passbook that said exactly who he was and exactly where he was supposed to be...my father wasn't where he was supposed to be, and the police got him.

Dieter's parents, Ernst & Liesa Krakow: "The Krakows" About 1922

We didn't actually call them police; we called them "Chain Dogs." They were the military police. The Chain Dogs got him because my father made the mistake of going to downtown Berlin, and that's where they stopped him, checked his passbook, and saw that he overstayed his vacation. They told him he had two choices. The first was: they would hang him on the next light pole. The second choice was: he would be sent to the front line. He chose to go to the front line...Breslau. But the Russians were already in Breslau, and there was a lot of fighting going on there. Once he was in Breslau, the Russians caught him, and they sent him to a prison in Siberia. The Red Cross later told us that my father died in a prison in Siberia.

I think it was May of 1945 when the war was over, and they dissolved the military school. All the teachers had left, and there we were, about 150 of us who were from eight to fourteen years old, and we were in need of food and housing. None of us were any older. Anyone who was over fourteen had already been drafted.

The military school in Bavaria was closed, and to earn enough money to live after the war, Dieter went to area farms, offering his services as hired help. After about the third stop, he got a job. His chores included bringing the cows out to the pasture in the morning, and bringing them home again at night. This left a lot of time for him think. He often thought about his family, and going home, but he also thought about juggling. He always wanted to try his hand at juggling. Although he wanted to learn how to juggle, he couldn't even try to learn because he had no juggling props, so he improvised by juggling with stones and dried cow pies. After seeing the look on my face, he quickly pointed out, "Well…the cow pies looked like plates."

That was in 1945. The war had ended, but there was no mail or telephones. It took nearly a year before the Red Cross found him and told him that his father had died in Russia. His mother died in 1942. His stepmother was still alive in Karow, but there was no way to get back there. And then one day, the local authorities arranged for him to take a bus with a local soccer team that was going to play a ball game in Berlin, and Dieter was finally able to go home. They gave him some money, put him on the bus, and sent him to Berlin. Dieter told the driver to let him off at the train station, and he knew how to get to Karow from there, which he did. He made a surprise visit to his stepmother. And it was a big surprise. She had no idea where he was or how he was. He stayed with her for about six months, but it was not easy. This was in East Berlin. If you know your history, you recall food was in very short supply in East Berlin, and it led to the Berlin Airlift. Dieter said, "It was tough on her. She already had two kids to feed."

Dieter then decided to contact his uncle Otto, who lived in downtown Berlin. Uncle Otto was a comedy juggler, who was known as "Little Knox." He also had another juggler uncle known as King Repp. King Repp was also a very good juggler, but that's another story.

Dieter told Uncle Otto that he wanted to be a juggler and Uncle Otto said, "Well, we will first have to see if you have any talent." Dieter admitted that he did not have any talent, and when that became apparent to Uncle Otto, his uncle told him he should become a shoemaker. Dieter said, "To prove him wrong I would get up at night and secretly practice." He said, "I even got brave enough to go outside and juggle on the street, and quite often cars would stop and watch me." He was still living with his stepmother at that time.

"King Repp"

Dieter's juggling progressed...slowly at first...but he eventually showed some significant signs of considerable talent. After a few weeks, Uncle Otto could see the improvement, and he offered Dieter a chance to live with him and became his apprentice. Dieter then went to live with his uncle Otto and aunt Klara in Berlin, and in time he learned the juggling technique. Before long, he was so good he signed a contract to work with Uncle Otto as a team. The duo was known as "The Two Krakows." The contract was for three years, but the act went over so well the two worked together another five years. By the time he was thirteen, Dieter learned what would become his signature trick: "The Cups and Saucers." It won much praise in Berlin, and soon led to signing a contract with Ringling Bros. and Barnum & Bailey Circus, "The Greatest Show on Earth."

Dieter didn't originate the Cups and Saucers routine. He thinks that it was originated by a juggler from Augsburg, Germany, whose name was Ferry Mader. The routine was adopted by a couple of others, including Sigi Manulescu and Rudy Horn. Manulescu did it while standing and balancing on a large rolling globe. Horn did it while riding a unicycle. Not to be outdone, Dieter did the Cups and Saucers while riding a unicycle and balancing on a slack wire.

Rudy Horn was about a year older than Dieter. He was born in Nuremburg, Germany, and he started juggling when he was only nine years old. Dieter told me that in the early days, Rudy Horn was his idol. Rudy was from a circus family. He was a year older than Dieter, and he was already causing quite a stir when he was only nine years old. Rudy made his first public appearance performing with his grandfather. The nine-year-old would stand on his grandfather's head while both Rudy and the elderly man juggled clubs. But the highlight of the act was the finishing juggle where Rudy would do the Cups and Saucers routine.

Dieter started doing the act when he was thirteen years old, but developing the technique was only part of it. Dieter said, "It took a long time to learn, and even longer to make something out of it, to sell it to the audience." Once Dieter perfected the Cups and Saucers routine, that routine became his signature routine.

In the early days, there were a number of little things that needed to be fine-tuned in their act. For one, Uncle Otto saw the need to give Dieter the stage name "Tasso." He told Dieter to use the last name Tasso because the word Tasso phonetically sounds like the word for cup in nearly all of the European languages. So from then on, Dieter Krakow became Dieter Tasso. Uncle Otto also knew that the clubs and cabarets where they worked needed the acts to maintain a specific block of time, to keep the entire show on time. They wanted the individual acts to run about ten or twelve minutes, no more. So, whenever Dieter perfected a new juggle, Uncle Otto would remove one of his. There is also an old show-biz adage regarding closing: "Close on a high point and then leave while they still want more."

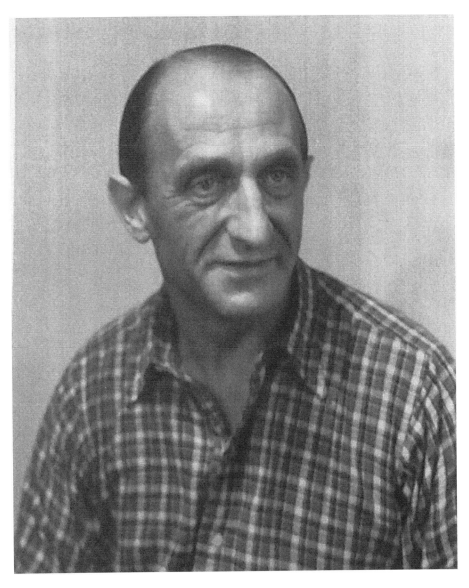

Uncle Otto: "Little Knox"

Timeline #4, 1947 to 1952: Working In Berlin

In September of 1947, when Dieter was thirteen years old, he did his first professional booking in front of an audience. One of the tricks they did went like this: Uncle Otto would be wearing a hat, and he had a cigar in his mouth. He would juggle three clubs. Then Dieter would step in front of Otto, and one by one take over juggling the clubs. In between juggling the clubs, he would also grab Otto's hat and plop it on his own head, and then he would take the cigar right out of Otto's mouth and start smoking it himself. Then Otto would step in front of Dieter, and one by one take over juggling the clubs again. He would take the hat, and put it back on his own head, grab the cigar out of Dieter's mouth, and put it back in his own mouth.

In Berlin they mostly worked one-nighters in cabarets, nightclubs, and for various group functions in need of entertainment. With the addition of the cups and saucer trick, they eventually were good enough to work the elegant Friederichstadt Palast. It was there, in 1952, that Henry Ringling North saw Dieter perform his Cups and Saucers routine—at the Friederichstadt Palast in Berlin—and he was so impressed he wanted to sign Dieter to perform in the center ring for the Ringling Bros. and Barnum & Bailey Circus in America. Henry Ringling North sent his business card backstage to Dieter with a note saying that he would like to talk with him about performing in America, but he got called away before Dieter was able to meet with him.

Dieter was only eighteen years old, and he wasn't all that eager to leave home and move to another country with another language, so he decided not to call Henry Ringling North as requested. But it wasn't very long before Ringling had an agent contact Dieter about the possibility of him coming to America to perform center ring for The Greatest Show on Earth.

The original 3,000-seat Friederichstadt Palast

Timeline #5, 1952: Coming to America

In January of 1952, the Italian ocean liner *Vulcania* sailed from Genoa, Italy, to New York, and an eighteen-year-old Dieter and his uncle Otto and aunt Klara were on board. The *Vulcania* was built in 1926, and Dieter recalled that it was pretty slow. It had a maximum speed of nineteen knots. That is half the speed of the *Queen Mary*. Dieter said, "It was an Italian ship, and it seemed even longer because every day they served spaghetti." He added, "But they also had bottles of wine on the table, which made eight days of eating spaghetti a little more tolerable for an eighteen-year-old boy." But it gets worse. Once they were in New York, Dieter spoke very little English, and he had trouble ordering food in a restaurant. I know this is probably going to sound like that old Henny Youngman "Apple Pie and Coffee" joke. Dieter only knew how to order "spaghetti." For another two weeks, the eighteen-year-old didn't want to be a problem, so he would order spaghetti. He told me he hasn't had spaghetti since.

(The actual "'Apple Pie and Coffee'" joke is below.)

Speaking of Henny Youngman, during the interview, Dieter and I got to talking about Henny's "Apple Pie and Coffee" joke and Dieter told me he worked with Henny several times. He said the last time, Henny was doing his routine from a wheelchair. I said, "That doesn't surprise me. Henny was a heck of a promoter and a very hard-working guy." I also knew Henny quite well. One time "The King of the One-liners" invited me to sit at his table when they roasted actor Ernest Borgnine. I had to turn him down. I had a firm booking the same day, and I was locked into my booking.

Another time, when I was booked in Newark, New Jersey, Henny invited me to go to the Friars Club with him. Even though my Newark booking was just twenty minutes from New York, once again my booking in Newark and the Friars Club lunch in New York were at the same time, and I had to turn him down. I'll never forget it. The guy who booked me for the Newark luncheon, did so after hearing my demo tape. Then he also acted as the emcee at the banquet and actually used three of the jokes he heard on my demo tape...prior to introducing me. He was oblivious to the fact the whole idea of a demo tape is to demonstrate my routine.

The MS *Vulcania* arrived in New York in early January of 1952. If you are old enough to recall, on January 14, 1952, NBC's *Today Show* debuted with host Dave Garraway and Jack Lescoulie. On April 1, 1952, Dieter Tasso debuted at New York's Madison Square Garden, and sixty years later both NBC and Dieter Tasso are still in business. Dieter said, "The first performances at Madison Square Garden were hard. I was used to smaller theaters, and I was young, and on the other side of the ocean in another country, and they spoke another language. Sometimes I just wanted to just go home, but we had a contract." He was booked at Madison Square Garden for six weeks, and then he was booked at the Boston Garden for a week.

Again, while Dieter didn't originate the Cups and Saucers routine, he was the first one to take it to America. And Dieter quickly learned that if you just do straight juggling for twenty minutes, they start throwing tomatoes at you. He said, "That's why, little by little, I added the comedy."

18

(The "'Apple Pie and Coffee" joke)

An immigrant man got a job in New York, but he could speak almost no English, so he couldn't order food at the diner during his lunch break. To alleviate the problem, he had a friend teach him how to say, "Apple pie and coffee."

He practiced the phrase over and over and that's what he would proudly order day after day. This worked well for a while, but apple pie and coffee every day soon got old, so he had his friend teach him how to say, "Ham and cheese sandwich." He then repeated this over and over until he could say it clearly.

The next day when the waitress asked what he wanted he said, "Ham and cheese sandwich." The waitress said, "You want that on white, whole wheat, or rye?" There was a long pause, and then the guy said, "Apple pie and coffee."

The Italian liner Vulcania

Timeline #6, 1952–1953: Life under the Big Top

After the shows in New York and Boston, Dieter boarded a train and headed out to perform "under the Big Top." After arriving, he recalled, he walked from the train to the circus grounds, and he saw the Big Top tent for the first time. He described the unique experience, saying: "The tent was out of view on the other side of a long hill. At first we could only see the top of the tent, but as we climbed farther and farther up the hill, we could see more and more of the tent, and as we climbed up the hill, the tent seemed to rise up out of the ground. It was huge. As we got closer, we started running because it was so exciting. The closer we got, the faster we would run, trying to see what it looked like." He added, "I get goose bumps just talking about it."

In 1952, the circus no longer traveled by truck. It traveled by train. There was one gigantic train system made up of three separate trains that brought the show to the various cities. The first section was the advance train for advertising and advance needs. This went out a week or so ahead of the other two circus train sections. The advance train carried the men needed to hang posters, do all of the advance promotions, and perform any advance setup that might be needed. The second section of the circus train was made up of twenty-two cars, which had the tents and the workers necessary to load and unload them. The third section was made up of twenty-eight cars, and it carried the people who erected the tents as well as the ushers and sideshow workers. The third section also had the sleeping cars for the performers and the crew.

Sleeping on the train was "classy" inasmuch as, the higher your class, the better your sleeping arrangements. The owner had a plush train car all to himself. Conversely, those on the other end of the spectrum had an entire cot all to themselves, and those on the lowest level often had to share a cot with someone of lesser class, who may have spent the day cleaning up after the elephants. There was most often a circus parade and the tent setup, which was a big draw. As a result, in a town of five thousand they would most likely play to as many as seven thousand.

For what it's worth…there's an old vaudeville-era joke about an old guy who spent his life as a circus employee in charge of cleaning up after the elephants. The guy had been with the circus, cleaning up after the elephants, all of his life. After all those years he was getting quite old and someone asks him why he doesn't retire. The old guy totally rejects the idea. The old guy says, "Are you kidding…and get out of show business?" That's just a joke, but to some extent it brings home the point: the circus and show business get into your blood.

In the past, Dieter had worked other venues, and at first, performing in the tent took some getting used to. He said, "You worked with three rings, and usually the other acts in the other rings were performing at the same time you were." The audience was spread out. There was the remoteness as well as the commotion of various setups going on elsewhere in the tent, and there were various vendors selling popcorn, balloons, and so on. It was much different from working a stage show. But he explained, "The audiences were great, and before long I learned how to work under those conditions." He added, "I was lucky. I was in the center ring."

He said, "I opened with some tennis rackets. They were known as 'Devil Sticks.' Then I did some top hat juggling and some cigar box juggling. It was all on the ground. The progression then went to the slack wire where I did my Cup and Saucer routine." But I should remind the reader, if you saw Dieter work at the *Tommy Bartlett Show*, he was doing the Cups and Saucers while standing on the stage. Under the Big Top he did the same Cups and Saucers routine, only instead of standing on the stage, he stood on one foot, balancing on a slack wire, and he tossed the cups and saucers to his head with the other foot. He would stack seven (sometimes as many as ten) cups and saucers on his head. His record was twelve cups and saucers while on the slack wire, and once he did an amazing stack of fourteen while practicing on the ground.

There are so many interesting stories in the life of this variety entertainer. Like the time back in 1952 when Ringling took the circus to pre-Castro Cuba, and in the audience was the Cuban president, Fulgencio Batista, who stayed after the show to personally greet and thank the performers.

The Ringling Show goes to pre-Castro Cuba in 1952 (Dieter far right)

Timeline #7, 1954: It's a Small World

Dieter spent a lot of time on the road. He traveled all over the United States, up into Canada, down into Cuba and South America, all over Europe, up into Scandinavia, down to Australia, and into North Africa. Dieter would be the first to tell you that it's a big world, and then add, "...but sometimes it's a small world. When Uncle Otto and I worked shows in Berlin, there were two cute girl tumblers, known as The Two Grigorys. They often worked the same shows that we worked, and I found out that one of them lived about a block and a half away from me.

"I was sixteen years old, and found myself attracted to her. Her name was Ursula Frimberger, but they called her 'Uschi.' My aunt had a little dog, and she always made me walk the dog. I wasn't too crazy about walking the dog, but one day I came up with a little plan. I would walk the dog on the street in front of Uschi's house, hoping that she would be outside and I could then 'accidently' run into her. Sometimes I would walk the dog four or five times a day in front of Uschi's house, trying to accidently run into her. One day it actually worked. She was outside and we talked.

"That was in 1950, before I came to America. And then one day in 1954, when I had been with Ringling Brothers for a couple of years, they hired four women tumblers who called themselves 'The Four Whirlwinds.' And it turned out that two of The Four Whirlwinds were the two Grigory tumblers that I worked with in Berlin. I'm on the other side of the world, and I run into her again. She was my first love and we eventually got engaged, but it only lasted through the season, because in 1955 I left Ringling and she stayed. I would visit her from time to time, and we are still good friends. Matter of fact, she lives in Sarasota, Florida, where I live. I saw her awhile ago at a birthday party for Evi Kelly, Emmett Kelly's widow. And then, once again, it's a small world. Evi Kelly was the other member of The Two Grigorys, the acrobatic troupe that we worked with in Berlin, in the early '50s." The duo eventually added two members and they called themselves "The Four Whirlwinds."

The Four Whirlwinds:
Left: Seigrid Duille, top center: Evi Kelly,
bottom center: Uschi Frimberger, right: Ulla Duille

Evi Gebhardt-Kelly was born in Leipzig, Germany, and moved to Berlin at a young age. She also spent her childhood among the ruins of her war-ravaged country, and although she did not come from a circus family, at the age of fifteen she took advantage of acrobatic and circus training in Berlin. She then formed the acrobatic partnership with her friend, Ursula "Uschi" Frimberger. Later, Evi and Uschi were joined by two sisters, and the four girls formed a new act they called "The Four Whirlwinds." The name reflected the speed of their acrobatic performance. Their act took them to entertainment venues and circuses throughout Europe. While they were in Copenhagen, they were discovered by John Ringling North. Shortly after that, they came to America on the *Queen Mary* and opened at Madison Square Garden. Evi joked, "I came over here in 1954, I married Emmett in 1955, and by 1957 I had two little girls… so I guess I was somewhat of a whirlwind." To this day, Evi and Uschi have remained friends.

Regarding Dieter and Emmett: With encouragement from the circus management, Emmett would wander around while the other acts were performing. His signature gag was to sweep up the circle of light that the spotlight made on the floor. If you're old enough, you remember that. No doubt Emmett's second-best bit would have to be when Dieter was balancing on one leg on the slack wire, and Emmett, in his sad hobo face, would stand nearby with a small sack, ready to catch Dieter if he fell. A film crew flew in from California and was in the process of doing a story on Emmett's career, but Emmett died on March 28, 1979. The filming was never completed.

The Whirlwinds
Evi Gebhardt-Kelly, Ursula "Uschi" Frimberger, and
sisters Ulla and Seigrid Duille
Photo from the Illinois State University, Milner Library,
Special Collections

The Second-Greatest Show on Earth

Many people would arrive early and stay late to watch the precision involved in setting up and tearing down the Big Top tent, as they moved the circus from place to place on the circus trains, which has been called "The Second-Greatest Show on Earth." It all started before the last performance even began. As the need for items in the show ended, that item was loaded onto the train. Each piece was then loaded into the assigned box, and put into the assigned wagon each time the show moved on. As each load was completed, the wagon was coupled to others and towed to the railroad siding. Six hours after the show began, the train was ready to roll again to its next event location.

In the early 1950s, Ringling Brothers was still entertaining the public under the Big Top tents. The two exceptions were New York (Madison Square Garden) and Boston (Boston Garden). Since the tent and its rigging were not required in these cities, they were played consecutively.

Loading the elephants

As I stated earlier, three separate trains were required. The first train was made up of wagons on flat cars, and the second train was made up of stock cars. These were followed by a third train, which was made up of a string of sleeping cars used by the performers. Dieter told about the time the train he was on stopped to water and feed the animals. While the train was stopped, a couple of the younger guys stepped off the train and ran up a big hill, and then wandered to the other side, never thinking that the train would leave without them...but it did. Knowing the third section of the train would be coming along soon, they waited on the track, flagged the train down when it came along, and then they jumped on board.

The years of the bigger circuses performing under Big Top tents were coming to a close largely as a result of a horrible disaster in Hartford, Connecticut, on July 6, 1944, when 168 people died in a blaze during a performance of the Ringling Brothers and Barnum and Bailey Circus. Many of the fatalities were a result of people being trampled by other people who were rushing to get out. It was further complicated when some spectators refused to leave the burning tent until they had located their friends and family members. Among the 6,700 people who survived the horrible blaze were the well-known circus clown, Emmett Kelly, and a thirteen-year-old boy by the name of Charles Nelson Reilly.

The Beginning of the End of the Big Top (1944)

168 people die in Big Top Fire; Hartford, Connecticut, July 6, 1944.

The End of the Big Top Era

In **1956** the Ringling Bros. and Barnum & Bailey Circus gave its last performance in the Big Top. John Ringling North declared that the tented circus as it exists today is a thing of the past, and a seven-page story in the July 30, 1956, edition of Life magazine said, "The Big Top Bows Out Forever." In July of 1956, midway through a season dogged by labor troubles, wet weather, and accidents, the Ringling Bros. and Barnum & Bailey Circus canceled the rest of the season. Two weeks earlier the King Brothers Circus closed, and in that same year the Clyde Beatty Circus went bankrupt. The decline continued throughout the 1960s. Surviving circuses were very small, and worst of all, they had few superstars who could perform the crowd-pleasing feats. Many circus people, who had spent their entire life with the circus, were suddenly out of work.

Dieter told about how, after so many people were put out of work, talent agent Al Dobritch heard about it and had an idea. He took a small airplane and intercepted the Ringling train at one of its aforementioned "stops to water the animals." Dobritch then boarded the stopped train and booked a dozen acts. He told them, "You will be on *The Ed Sullivan Show* next week." And as you can imagine, they were all thrilled. The only problem was that Dobritch had not talked to Ed Sullivan. And when he tried to reach Sullivan, he couldn't. Ed Sullivan was out of the country. And when he finally did reach Sullivan, Dobritch told him that the Ringling Bros. Circus had just ended the show midseason and he had their best performers available to work *The Ed Sullivan Show*. Well, it was like one of those old Andy Hardy movies with Mickey Rooney and Judy Garland. Ed Sullivan loved the idea. He postponed the acts that had been scheduled, and on July 29, 1956, *The Ed Sullivan Show* aired with all twelve of the replacement circus acts, including

Emmett Kelly (clown), Tito (acrobat), The Cordons (whip act), The Reberte Trio (knockabouts), Miss Mara (trapeze), The Two Marilex (plate spinners), Pinito de Oro (aerialists), The Burtons (hand-balancing), Al De Gong (chimpanzees), Dschapur & Rutha (jump act), Tonito (wire artist), and Adnos (jugglers). It turned out to be one of the highest rated Sullivan shows prior to the shows featuring Elvis and the Beatles.

Sullivan regularly booked circus acts after that. As for the fate of the circus...they discontinued that season, and discontinued using the portable tents. There was also a change of ownership, and when the circus resumed, it started working only at venues such as sports stadiums and arenas with the seating already in place. the Big Top Tent era, at least for the big circuses, had come to an end.

In addition to circus acts, Al Dobritch was Dieter's agent. He also handled the Wallendas and other top acts. Al Dobritch was also involved with the Tripoli Circus and Circus Circus in Vegas. His family was associated with the circus for 250 years.

On March 11, 1971, Alexander Al Dobritch rented a room at the Mint Hotel in Las Vegas, and from a window in that room, he for some reason jumped to his death. He was sixty years old.

Timeline #8, 1955–1969: After the "Big Top" and the Ringling Years

In **1955**, after the Ringling days, there were twenty years of traveling and shows. As the saying goes, "New York had The Copacabana and The Latin Quarter, and in Boston there was Blinstrub's. Dieter worked Blinstrub's several times, and the list of big stars that had appeared at Blinstrub's in those days was extremely impressive. It included Robert Goulet, Wayne Newton, Al Martino, The Four Aces, The Four Lads, Dionne Warwick and Joan Weber. Joan Weber only had the one big hit, but if you grew up in those days you probably will remember "Let Me Go Lover." For what it's worth, I found it interesting that the song was originally called "Let Me Go Devil," but Mitch Miller had the lyrics rewritten and changed to "Let Me Go Lover."

Singer Johnny Mathis may have been Blinstrub's best buy. As I understand it, in 1955, Johnny Mathis signed a contract for $600 a week. Approximately one month later, Johnny Mathis hit it big with the song "Wonderful Wonderful," and his price shot up to several thousand a week, but Mathis had signed a contract a few months prior for $600 a week and it had to be honored. The McGuire Sisters were a big attraction in the mid-1950s. They also booked Gordon McCrae, the Mills Brothers, Guy Lombardo, Johnny Ray, Connie Francis, Frankie Lane, Eddie Fisher, and a juggler by the name of Dieter Tasso.

On Dieter's first booking there in 1955, he worked with Pat Boone. Boone had just had two big hits on the Dot label, and Pat Boone and Dieter Tasso got along great. They were the same age. Both were born in 1934. Dieter told about the night Pat Boone wanted to switch sport coats. Pat Boone had been wearing a black tuxedo, but for some reason on this day he wanted to wear Dieter's brightly colored sport jacket. At the time, Dieter also wore white buck shoes on stage, and he said, "The next time I saw Pat Boone, he was wearing a brightly colored sport jacket and white buck shoes."

In **1956,** Dieter was booked on *The Ed Sullivan Show* with Gary Cooper and Burt Lancaster, and *The Patti Page Show* with Julius LaRosa and one of my favorites, Johnny Puleo and the Harmonica Rascals.

In **1957** Dieter was booked on The Jackie Gleason All Star Circus Review with Emmett Kelly and Hugh O'Brian. He was also booked for the Toronto Sports Show with Nat King Cole, and he did a thirty-nine-day traveling gig with Gene Autry's Stage Show. Autry took him from gig to gig in his D-18 twin-engine Beechcraft airplane. Bookings in 1957 included The Jackie Gleason Buffalo Shows and some dates with the Clyde Brothers Circus in Syracuse, and The Fort Worth Shrine Circus, as well as The Hamilton Standard Circus in Hartford, Connecticut, which was thirteen years after the horrible Ringling circus tent fire in Hartford.

In **1958** he was on *The Ed Sullivan Show* again, with Sam Levenson and The Tom Packs Circus. He worked Shrine Circuses in New Orleans, St. Louis, Atlanta, and Omaha. He also worked the Minneapolis Auto Show with Pat Boone and Peggy Lee, The Cristiani Brothers Circus, and The Atlanta Shrine Circus.

Recalling his **1959** venture, Dieter said, "I traveled with Circus Scott throughout Sweden in 1959 and that was an interesting year. Circus Scott was a five-month run in Sweden. We went all the way up to

Kiruna, which is Sweden's northernmost city. Kiruna is above the Arctic Circle. That means that in the summer it never gets dark, and in the winter it never gets light. I remember one day in the early evening during the summer solstice we climbed a small hill at sunset, and we watched the sun set. But when the sun got down to the horizon, it just stopped, and then it moved a little bit to the right, and started to rise again. It never went below the horizon."

Circus Scott is a Swedish circus, founded in 1937 by brothers Charles, Herman, Bruno, and Natini Bronett. The brothers were famous clowns. Bruno's wife, Käte Bronett, took over Circus Scott when the brothers died at an early age. In 1959, Circus Scott was managed by Käte Bronett's son, Francois Bronett. It was under his management that Circus Scott became one of the greatest circuses in Europe. During his career, Bronett evolved into one of the most competent circus personalities. Prince Rainier of Monaco asked Bronett to be the artistic director of the Monte-Carlo Circus, but this next thing I'm going to tell you was before all that.

Francois Bronett had grown up in the circus, but in 1959 he was new to management. For some reason, at the end of the 1959 Circus Scott season in Sweden, Francois Bronett got the idea to assemble a small circus and take it down to Algeria in northern Africa. Normally that might have been OK, but this was during the terrible Algerian Revolution. If that revolution isn't familiar to you, I will point out that the revolution went on from 1954 to 1962, and it was estimated that from 960,000 to 1,500,000 people were killed during that revolution. The French were kicked out, but for some reason, Francois Bronett wanted in.

Dieter said, "There were rifles and machine guns and bombings, and the police would search everyone. The police would even line the circus people up against the wall and search us for weapons. We were doing two one-hour shows per day, and to complicate things more, there were curfews that we had to work around. But surprisingly, we sold out almost every day. The reason being, none of the big shows, like Holiday on Ice, would come down there during the revolution. The people were five years into a revolution, and they needed some form of escape from the horrors of the life they were living each day. We set up in the cities of Oran and Algiers, and we stayed there for about six weeks, and believe it or not, we sold out nearly every show...but I would never do it again. After we left, we did some shows in Marseille and Nice in France, and as it turned out...we did better in Oran and Algiers in Africa."

Uncle Otto died, at age sixty-three, while Dieter was in Africa.

In **1960** Dieter married Joyce Kuhn. They met back when they were with Ringling Bros. and Barnum & Bailey Circus. Joyce did an aerialist trapeze act. She got her start as an aerialist with Captain Eddie Kuhn's Wild Animal Circus. Captain Eddie was her step-father. Joyce was a circus performer all her life, and after the wedding she toured South America and Europe with The Cristiani Brothers Circus. They both had their own circus careers. Joyce did a trapeze act and Dieter did his slack wire Cups and Saucers routine.

The years **1961, 1962, and 1963** included more travels with The Cristiani Brothers Circus, and dates with The Alhambra Temple Shrine Circus and The Harold Brothers Circus.

On **January 5, 1964,** Dieter was once again booked on *The Ed Sullivan Show* with Count Basie and Jane Powell. In the years **1964, 1965, and 1966**, while he was still in his 30s, Dieter and his father-in-law (Captain Eddy Kuhn, Joyce's step-father) bought a small "forty-miler" type carnival on borrowed money. With long hours and hard work, they were able to sell it at a profit. Dieter then bought one of the first inflatable "Moonwalk" attractions on his own. It was the third Moonwalk made by the company. The Moonwalk was part of an evolution of inflatables that also included the inflatable mat that fire fighters use to catch people who are trapped on the upper floors of burning buildings.

In **1967,** Dieter and Joyce decided to divorce. Dieter said, "We were too young to get married. We didn't argue or anything like that, but our careers took us in different directions, and we just agreed to get a divorce." And in 1967, Dieter started working with the Harlem Globetrotters. For seven years he provided entertainment before each game and again during halftime. While he was with the Globetrotters he traveled all over the United States, South America, Europe, and Australia. In those years he was still doing the slack wire, but on a smaller slack wire rigging, and he was also doing a plate spinning act.

In **1968,** Dieter met Consuelo "Connie" Armstrong. She performed a trapeze act on a portable rigging that worked well in night clubs. Those night club bookings were known as one-nighters. Dieter and Connie got married in October of 1968, and on January 16, 1969, Connie was driving through North Dakota on icy roads. Her car slid into an oncoming truck. The truck nearly cut the car in half and Connie died instantly. She had been en route from Chicago to Montana to be with Dieter, who had been traveling with the Harlem Globetrotters at the time. Dieter said, "I talked to her before she left, because I didn't want her to drive to Montana from Chicago, through Wisconsin, Minnesota, and North Dakota, in January. I told her it would be better if she waited until we got to our next booking, which was in the South, but she decided that she would make the drive anyway. After he was notified of the accident, Dieter went to North Dakota to escort Connie's body on a flight back to Chicago.

Circus people have always been very close, and two of Dieter and Connie's great circus friends, Ruth and Frank Clark (professionally known as Francarro & Estreleta), met him at the Chicago O'Hare Airport when he flew in from North Dakota on the plane that carried Connie's body.

About Connie, Ruth Clark said, "Connie was a very accomplished aerialist, and did difficult tricks with class, ease, and with very pleasing projection. She was a dear friend. She and I practiced our individual trapeze acts together many times, in Chicago, between club dates, fairs, circus, etc. She was my maid of honor at our helicopter wedding in London, Ontario, in 1966. She was a beautiful person and a beautiful performer."

Consuelo "Connie" Armstrong

Regarding his wife, Irene, Dieter told me that in 1947/48 she studied to become a ballet dancer. Here I should probably point out that Dieter still has a bit of a German accent, and when he said "ballet dancer," I heard "belly dancer." I'm glad he corrected me before this went to press.

Irene was working with her stepson, Heinz Pichler Jr., who was the son of Heinz Pichler Sr. Irene had married Heinz Pichler Sr. in Germany, a few years after Pichler lost his wife to cancer. Irene, Heinz Junior, Junior's wife, Linda, and his sister, Sylvia, all came to the US in 1965 and were part of the Mills Brothers Circus based in Ohio. They had performed a lot in Germany, as well as all over the world. In the circus world Heinz Sr. was known as "Jolly" and his son was known as "Jolly, Jr." For the reader who might be a real circus buff, this father/son team, plus The Great Barton and Franz Furtner (known as: "Unus"), were responsible for making the "One Finger Handstand" famous. I saw video of Unus doing the One Finger Handstand. He was quite a talent and quite a showman. I found no video of Jolly doing it, but several of the people I interviewed also raved about Jolly's talent and ability. They thought Jolly was as good as Unus, or better. Jolly Jr. also did the One Finger Handstand, and Jolly Jr. also traveled with Circus Vargas. I'm told, but can't verify, Circus Vargas suggested that Jolly Jr. change his show name to Dante.

As I mentioned above, Irene had worked with, and then she eventually married, Heinz Pichler. Unfortunately, he too became very sick. For several years Irene took care of him until he died. After that Irene and her stepson, Heinz Jr., and stepdaughter, Sylvia, continued a three-person act that was variously known as "The Henrys" or "The Shappis." Irene was an acrobat in the group, and she did some great tumbling and a handstand while on a moving bicycle. She was also hidden inside a small piano that Jolly built for a comedy routine they did. While inside, she was the "motor" propelling and steering this little piano that seemingly moved around on its own.

Dieter said he had met Irene, but he didn't really know her. He got to know Irene better in 1969 at a mutual booking for the Allen-Bradley Christmas party in Milwaukee. The Miller Brewery people invited the cast of the Allen-Bradley show to a luncheon where Irene and Dieter sat at the same table. He jokingly said, "I met her at a brewery. She was sitting under a keg of beer." The Allen-Bradley show lasted about a week. Afterward, Dieter went to Sarasota, and Irene and The Shappis went to a booking in Puerto Rico. While Irene was away, he decided to write to her. He didn't write a letter, he wrote a post card…that he didn't mail. He carried it for several days. It was still so soon after Connie's death. You probably suspect what came next. He eventually mailed the post card, and Irene wrote back, and Dieter and Irene became friends.

Coming to America: (1965)
From the left: Irene and Heinz Pichler Sr. (Jolly) behind the baby.
Heinz Pichler Jr. (Jolly Jr.) and wife, Linda, with baby in the middle.

On Death, Friends, and Friendships

Acquaintances and friends are mingled in the mix of people around us, but our true friends will still be there when our mere acquaintances have left. Connie's death was sudden and brutal. Previously I mentioned Connie and Dieter's friends, Ruth and Frank Clark, and how they helped Dieter in the dark days immediately after Connie's death. It may sound trite for me to point out that "life goes on," but life does go on. The days, and then weeks, and then months passed, and then a mutual friend of theirs, Irene Fossett, saw the void in Dieter's life, and the void in the life of her longtime friend, Irene Pichler, who also had lost her spouse. After Irene Pichler returned from Puerto Rico, Irene Fosset took action.

Both Dieter and Irene were still in their thirties, and each had lost a spouse, so their mutual friend, Irene Fossett, decided to play cupid. She invited them to her house for a small get-together. Neither of them knew that the other was invited. As the song from the Muppet Movie goes, "There's not a word yet, for old friends who've just met." The night could not have gone better.

As planned, Irene's stepson, Heinz Jr., brought her, and then left. As they had hoped, Dieter quickly offered to take Irene home. There is a Robert Louis Stevenson line: "Marriage is a friendship that is recognized by the police." That night, the soon-to-be "old friends" experienced the birth of a beautiful forty-year friendship, soon to be recognized by the police.

Irene

Timeline #9, 1970–1975: Cruise Ships and the TSS *Fairwind* Disaster

Dieter was hired by many cruise ship lines during the years from 1970 to 1975, and Irene always enjoyed the serenity of the cruise. He worked cruise ships in the winter. Cruise lines included the Holland American Line and the Carnival Cruise Line. The first ship he was booked on was the *Song of Norway*, which coincidently was the first ship of the Royal Caribbean Line, and he also worked on the TSS *Fairwind*, which was part of the Sitmar Cruise Ship Line. Dieter said,

> There were usually three acts. One was like mine and it went first, then a singer was second, and the third was usually a comedian. They were usually well-known entertainers. Ships had a big stage below where we did two shows. And most often there was also a lounge show above. One time a cruise director asked me if juggling would work up in the lounge, so I took a look at it. It had a low ceiling, but I was able to make it work.

> Working the lounge was an evening thing and most often the captain would come to see the show. He seemed to love my act, because when I was done he would stand up and applaud. Well, there must be an unwritten rule that if the captain stands up and gives you a standing ovation, everyone has to stand up and give you a standing ovation. I kinda liked that.

> Performing on a cruise ship usually involved switching ships. We did several shows because all the passengers

couldn't fit into one show, so we did half a week, and then we had to switch ships because, by then, everybody had seen the act. Then we had to fly (usually to an island), and get on some other ship. Most often on these flights there were four or five of us in a small airplane. Sometimes we would fly into tropical rains so heavy that the windshield wiper on the plane couldn't work fast enough. One time our pilot was very young, and we were flying in heavy rain for a long time. Finally the pilot said that he couldn't find the island (Saint Thomas Island). After a while, I suggested he should get down out of the clouds and fly lower, and if he sees any land...land, even if it is the wrong island. He flew lower, and all of a sudden, we saw an island. Fortunately, it was Saint Thomas.

Another time we headed out to get on board our new ship at the Panama Canal, but when we got there, the ship wasn't there. I called the office to find out what he wanted me to do. He checked and then told me that the ship was on the Pacific side of the Panama Canal and I needed to go to the other side. I asked him how I was supposed to get to the other side. He told me to take a taxi.

Taking a taxi in the middle of the Panamanian jungle is at least a little bit like taking a taxi in New York City or Chicago. The driver speaks very little English. However, that's where the similarity ends.

So we took a taxi through the jungle on a little two-lane road with potholes as big as my head. The old car that we were in didn't have any shock absorbers...probably because over its many, many years of service, it had hit too many

48

potholes on that road. I think we traveled about fifty miles. The temperature was over a hundred degrees, and there was no air-conditioning. When we got to the other side, once again there was no ship. We were told the ship was out on the ocean, but they told us that was OK. They said we could get to the ship on a small tender-boat that was taking the replacement crew members out to the ship. That sounded doable so we got on board and set out to sea.

We traveled for quite a while before we actually saw the ship, and as we got closer and closer, the Holland America ship seemed to get bigger and bigger. Normally, you board a ship at about the level of the main deck. You just walk from the dock to the ship on a very solid gangway, but we were down at the water level...looking up. The illusion was overwhelming as the gigantic ship towered over us. The ocean swells caused the smaller boat and the big ship to rise and fall independently of each other. I asked one of the crew how we would get on board...jokingly suggesting a rope ladder. He laughed, but he said, "Yes." And pretty soon someone from above lowered a rope ladder. Here's the problem with boarding by way of a rope ladder: it's difficult to get onto a rope ladder when, as I said, the two vessels are moving independently of each other, and the captain is concerned that the big boat will crush the little boat, or it will crush someone on the rope ladder, so they can't allow the two vessels to collide.

The replacement crew said they would stay on the smaller boat to help us make the transition to the ladder. Once on the rope ladder, the smaller boat backs off from the big boat, and you suddenly realize you are hovering over ocean swells on a rope…wondering how this happened. My wife had an additional concern. She envisioned herself clinging to the rope ladder as it was swung above the replacement crew members in the small boat, and she was wearing a short skirt. But our concerns were somewhat alleviated when they told us that we didn't have to actually climb the rope ladder. All we had to do is get on, and hang on, while they winched it up.

On another similar incident we flew to an island. I think the island was Trinidad. And once again we found out that the ship was on the other side of the island. The plane that brought us had gone back, but we were told there was a local guy we could hire to fly us. They said "local guy." They should have said "loco" guy.

He arrived without a shirt, and had been at some kind of party. He was too happy and appeared to have been drinking. They assured me he was an excellent pilot. All through the flight he was still very happy…way too happy! As he approached the mountain, he offered to show us that his plane could fly without the motor. We assured him that we didn't want to see it fly without the motor, but by then he was already throttling back to an idle. It had been difficult to talk over the roar of the motor, but now I wanted to hear it again. It turned out he was right. There was always a tremendous updraft at the mountain, and that updraft just carried the plane right over the top of the mountain. Before long, we landed safely on the other side and boarded our new ship.

Coincidently, Dieter's first cruise ship booking was on the first voyage of the *Song of Norway*, which was the first ship ever built for the new cruise line, "Royal Caribbean International." Working on a cruise ship usually had him working fourteen days, and then he got fourteen days off, and he was always able to take Irene.

Over a six year period (1970–1975), Dieter entertained on seventy-some Caribbean cruise ships. Cruise ships are always relaxing...except for the time there was "that explosion." It was Friday, November 28, 1975. They were aboard the seven-deck Italian ocean liner, T.S.S. *Fairwind* when the ship started on fire. It was about 2:00 p.m. when Dieter noticed that the engines stopped.

That had happened once before when he was on a cruise ship, so the concern was minimal. Still...he decided to check on Irene in their stateroom. When he got to the room he noticed that it was smoky in the room, and it was a different kind of smoke. Then came "the announcement" over the PA system...in Italian. Dieter said, "I don't speak Italian, but I knew the guy on the PA sounded very excited and out of breath."

And then came the announcement in English, asking everybody to go to their lifeboat station. More specifically, the announcer advised, "Go to your lifeboat station *fast*, but don't panic." One could spend a considerable amount of time analyzing that informative, but contradictory piece of advice. Dieter said, "We grabbed a few personal items and our lifejackets, and headed for the lifeboat station on the promenade deck."

When they arrived at the promenade deck, they found that the sliding glass door was locked. The "don't panic" advice was now getting much harder to follow. They were able to get it open, and they made it up to the promenade deck, where they stood for four hours watching the ship burning around them. Dieter said, "This was not a small fire. It was the real McCoy. At one point, we heard a dull thud, felt a concussion, and our ears popped. An elderly woman was thrown to the deck. I suspected that it was an explosion from a lower deck." At this point people more fully appreciated the "crash course" they were given shortly after they boarded, which had to do with "What to do, and what not to do, in case there is a fire."

Before long, two other cruise ships approached the *Fairwind* and circled, preparing to transfer passengers. Dieter recalled one of the ships coming to their aid was the *Norwegian Viking Star*. Passengers quickly gathered at the starboard rail and the ship just as quickly began to tilt heavily to the starboard side. Passengers were instructed to go to the other side of the ship, so they ran to the other side, and like a scene from an old Three Stooges movie, the ship then tilted too far the other way. Eventually the ship leveled off, and the fire was put out. As it turned out, the passengers would not have to abandon the ship after all.

Twenty cabins were damaged so badly they could not be used and all of the cabins without portholes couldn't be used. Over 75 percent of the passengers had to sleep in lounges, in hallways, or on deck. The *Fairwind* limped home on one engine, and arrived on Monday instead of Saturday.

TSS Fairwind

Dieter does not tell jokes. His delivery is more like an ongoing monologue. It's kind of like a conversation with the audience in a tone that is just above a mumble, that's followed by a nervous little laugh. On a cruise it involved things like the ship, or the ocean, or some island.

He would make comments like: "Don't be fooled if they tell you they visit nine islands in fourteen days. There's only one island. The ship just comes in from different directions." He would talk about the questions he gets. One guy wanted to know if the island is completely surrounded by water. There was the woman who wanted to know if the crew gets to sleep on the ship too.

Those lines, and many more like them, are the kind of thing that worked well on a cruise ship. However, you will note that while a cruise ship does have a movie theater, for obvious reasons they would never show a movie like *The Poseidon Adventure* or *Titanic*. That logic applies to jokes too. Below is the kind of joke that is funnier when you are high and dry and at home, and you are safely sitting in your recliner.*

"The captain of a cruise ship had a smart-aleck parrot that would expose all the magic tricks that were performed by the ship's lounge-show magician. The parrot would blurt out stuff like 'There's a secret trapdoor in the back...' Or he'd say, 'It's not magic. It's done with mirrors...' The parrot would make the magician look like a fool. As a result, the magician hated the parrot. Then one day the ship exploded and the magician and the parrot found themselves together in a lifeboat, adrift at sea. It was just the two of them, seated back-to-back and neither of them would speak to the other. For two days there was total silence as they floated aimlessly, and then in the morning of the third day the parrot relented. He turned and looked at the magician and said, 'OK... that was pretty good. Now bring the ship back!'"

*If you are reading this in the bathroom, please hurry, others may have to get in there.

Timeline #10, 1975: Variety Entertainment Has Peaked

The evolution of Variety Entertainment goes something like this: Juggling, String Puppets, and Acrobats. Then came: Minstrel Shows, The Circus, Vaudeville, and Medicine Shows. Then came the wonderful years of broadcast variety: early radio, early television, and primetime television, which flourished into the mid-1970s. This all pretty much came to an end nearly forty years ago. Some readers may not have been born or were very young when variety shows disappeared. For them I include the following description of variety entertainment from Wikipedia:

> *Variety show entertainment is made up of a variety of acts (hence the name), especially musical performances and sketch comedy, and it is normally introduced by a master of ceremonies. This variety format made its way from the Victorian era stage to radio and then to television. In several parts of the world variety TV remains popular and widespread. The format is basically that of vaudeville. In the US, former vaudeville performers such as the Marx Brothers, George Burns and Gracie Allen, W. C. Fields, and Jack Benny moved to sound movies, to radio shows, and then to television shows, including variety shows. In the US, shows featuring Perry Como, Milton Berle, Jackie Gleason, Bob Hope, and Dean Martin also helped to make the Golden Age of Television successful.*

> *From 1948 to 1971, The Ed Sullivan Show was one of CBS's most popular television series. Using his no-nonsense approach, Ed Sullivan allowed many acts from several different mediums to get their "fifteen minutes of fame." Sullivan was also partially*

responsible for bringing Elvis Presley and The Beatles to US promi-nence. Sid Caesar pioneered the television variety show format with a show called "Your Show of Shows" (1950–54) and "Caesar's Hour" (1954–57). ABC-TV aired "The Hollywood Palace," an hour-long show broadcast weekly (generally on Saturday night) from January 4, 1964, to February 7, 1970. That's where the Rolling Stones first appeared on American TV.

On television, variety reached its peak during the period of the 1960s and 1970s. With a turn of the television dial, viewers around the globe could variously have seen shows and occasional specials featuring Dinah Shore, Bob Hope, Bing Crosby, Perry Como, Andy Williams, Julie Andrews, The Carpenters, Olivia Newton-John, John Denver, Johnny Cash, Sonny and Cher, Carol Burnett, Rod Hull and Emu, Flip Wilson, Lawrence Welk, Glen Campbell, Donny and Marie Osmond, Barbara Mandrell, Judy Garland, The Captain and Tennille, The Jacksons, The Keane Brothers, Bobby Darin, Sammy Davis, Jr., Mary Tyler Moore, Dean Martin, Tony Orlando and Dawn, The Smothers Brothers, Danny Kaye. During the 1960s and 1970s, there were also numerous one-time variety specials featuring stars such as Shirley MacLaine, Frank Sinatra, Diana Ross, and Mitzi Gaynor, none of whom ever had a regular television series.

Timeline #11, 1980–1998: Winters at The Crazy Horse Saloon in Paris

Dieter spent eighteen winters in Paris working off-seasons at the Crazy Horse Saloon, which was quite challenging because the Crazy Horse stage was only eight feet tall and there was very little space between the top of the pile of dishware on his head, and the ceiling. They decided to make it easier by putting a lower stage in front of the big stage, but that was like standing on one of the front dinner tables. He said, "If I drop something I could kill someone." And there were many other great acts from America at The Crazy Horse Saloon in Paris, including two of my favorites, the unique and innovative comedy magician, Tom Mullica, and the lovable Señor Wences.

In Paris Dieter spoke English because the audience members were from various countries and English was the language that most people had as a second language. This worked well except for that time when the audience was mostly French butchers. Dieter decided to use the little French that he knew. After the show the owner, Alain Bernardin, came over to him and said, "Dieter, you know what you did wrong?" Dieter said, "No." The owner said, "You spoke French. You're not funny in French. You're funny in English."

Dieter pointed out, "It can get very confusing. Alain told me I'm not funny in French. German is my native language, but after all these years in America, I speak German with an English accent. My English isn't getting any better, and my German is getting worse. If this keeps up I think the day may come where I won't be able to speak at all. It could happen! At elite British men's clubs some of the members are so British they almost can't speak at all."

57

Crazy Horse Paris

DIETER TASSO

Dieter Caricature at Crazy Horse

The downside of trying to be funny

An old show business adage advises, "Never follow an animal act," especially if it's on a small stage in a crowded lounge at John Ascuaga's Nugget Casino, and the animal is an elephant with "the runs." Somehow it was both awkward and funny. Dieter remembered how eventually the stage crew was able to pretty much clean the stage, but not the air, and then he heard the stage manager call out, "Dieter, you're on!" And when the laughter and commotion finally stopped enough for him to be heard, Dieter opened with an absolutely beautiful ad-lib. Looking off stage, he yelled, "I can't believe you can train an elephant to do that for every show." The ad-lib got a big laugh and recaptured the crowd's attention, putting Dieter back in control of the awkward situation.

The elephant's owner, Jenda Smaha, was one of the best elephant trainers ever. His elephants also appeared on quite a few TV shows and in the James Bond movie *Diamonds are Forever*. The situation with Smaha's elephant was awkward, but occasionally there are far more dire circumstances where it is difficult to be funny, even though "to be funny" is why you were hired. I spent thirty years traveling nationally as a humorist on the banquet circuit. I vividly remember being booked the day the Space Shuttle Challenger crashed and the day of the San Francisco earthquake. I was booked the day they launched Desert Storm. While I was not booked on September 11, 2001, the day of the Twin Towers terrorist attack, I was booked two days later.

At one booking, a man had a heart attack during the banquet. He was given CPR, and after the ambulance crew wheeled him out of the banquet hall on a stretcher, I was introduced to go up and make the group laugh. At another banquet, the group's president informed the members that her doctor told her she had less than six months to live; after she left the podium, I was introduced to go up to the same podium and make them laugh.

These situations are very difficult. They are almost disrespectful. A good example would be the suicide of the owner of The Crazy Horse Saloon, Alain Bernardin. His body was carried by the ambulance crew, from his office, through the kitchen, and out the back door…in full view of the kitchen staff and those performers who were about to go out and entertain a full house.

Dieter mentioned the challenge he faced to perform so soon after the horrible Seaplane crash that killed four people in full view of the crowd that was taking their seats in the open-air grandstand at the *Tommy Bartlett Show*. He talked about the night, while traveling with the Harlem Globetrotters, when he was notified of the terrible automobile accident that had taken the life of his new bride, Connie, who had been driving to Montana to be with him.

As I said above, performing so closely after a tragedy can almost appear disrespectful, and then one night after I had entertained at a banquet, a woman came up to me and reached for my hand. She held it very tightly and said, "I want to thank you. Tonight is the first time that I have laughed since my husband died." She said, "It felt good." We hugged, and I also felt good that night while I made the long drive home. "What soap is to the body, laughter is to the soul."

Timeline #12, 1976: The *Tommy Bartlett Show* Years

While interviewing Tom Diehl about Dieter's thirty-five years at the *Bartlett Show*, I mentioned that I had just watched the video that was shot at Dieter's most recent trip back to Germany. He had performed for the Twentieth Anniversary Wintergarten show in Berlin. Actually, I had watched the video for the third time and I was impressed all over again. The man was a week or two away from turning seventy-nine years old, and he was in his sixty-fifth year of entertaining. He was doing physical stunts that I couldn't have done when I was twenty. He was speaking in German, which I don't understand, but I was laughing. I e-mailed a link of that video to a couple of friends of mine who were aware and interested in the fact that I was writing this book. In each case the friends didn't speak German, and in each case they commented on how hard they laughed, and they too didn't even know what he was saying.

This caused Tom Diehl to tell me a story his wife, Margaret, told about the Vietnamese manicurist who does her nails. The woman's mother was coming to the US from Vietnam to visit. Margaret invited the woman and her mother to be Margaret's guests at the show. The next time Margaret had her nails done, the woman raved about the show. Margaret was glad to hear that, and she asked what part her mother liked best. The woman said, "Dieter Tasso for sure." The woman said her mother laughed harder than she's ever seen her laugh, and Margaret then said, "I thought your mother didn't speak English." The woman said, "She doesn't speak a word of English, but she laughed hard at Dieter through his entire act." You might wonder why this happens. It's a combination of body language, facial expressions, proper pauses, and hearing the laughter of all those who understand what is being said.

Going back to 1977 and how it all started: Tom Diehl and Tommy Bartlett went to Las Vegas to see Dieter perform at the Hacienda

Casino. They were already aware of him, having seen him perform once in Madison Wisconsin. At the Hacienda, Dieter was doing his juggling routine: cigar boxes, wooden balls, colorful silk top hats, and then the finale, the Cups and Saucers. On the chance that some readers have not seen Dieter at the *Bartlett Show* and his routine, it typically goes like this:

> Early in his routine Dieter juggles cigar boxes and then goes to three colorful softball-sized wooden balls. He would drop one when taking it out of the bag, and it would crash onto the stage with a loud bang. Then he would intention-ally drop a second wooden ball with another loud bang, and to save face, he would suggest that it's part of the act. Then he would juggle the three wooden balls, and at one point he would send one of the balls high into the air and it would come down and bounce off his forehead with a loud...**crack!** And in his German accent he would grumble, "I hate this shtupid trick!" And under his breath he would complain about headaches. He would do this several times and then he would take the ball he had been banging off his forehead and bounce it on the stage. Guess what? It's rubber. It turns out only the other two balls are wooden. And as the rubber ball bounced off his forehead, Dieter would secretly bang the other two wooden balls together, which made the loud crack that the audience associated with the rubber ball that he was bouncing off his forehead.

The patter would continue as he would go about his various tricks while briefly stopping now and then to make small talk with the audience. Previously I described it as a: "...a conversation with the audience in a tone that is just above a mumble, that is followed by a nervous little laugh," and then whenever he gets a particularly good applause for some trick he did, he stops everything and says, "You like it? I do it again." It became his catchphrase and the title of this book.

In Dieter's signature trick he would alternately toss saucers and cups from his foot, and catch them on his head. First he would toss a saucer with his foot and catch it on his head. He would follow that by tossing a cup with his foot. That cup would land on the saucer he had just tossed and was waiting up there for its mate, the cup. Then he would put another saucer on his foot. He would toss it, and it would land on top of the cup and saucer already up there on his head. He would then add a third story to the stack, while feeling the need to pause and explain to the audience that he too is looking forward to the end of his performance, but he had to do the whole thing because it is part of his contract.

After the stack grows to four layers of cups and saucers, the next throw is intentionally too high, and the cup passes over his head. But to everyone's surprise, the cup doesn't crash on the floor behind him, because he makes a blind catch behind his back, which seems to even surprise Dieter. He follows it with the rather superfluous remark, "It's a good thing I was there." All formality is long gone as Dieter continues to share his intimate thoughts with the audience.

In his *Bartlett Show* performances he would stack five to eight sets of cups and saucers on his head, and after that he would put a lump of sugar on his toe and toss it into the top cup. The entire stack would then be topped with a teapot that was also tossed from his foot. Finally he would put a spoon on his foot and toss it into the teapot. Keep in mind, that he is now doing this trick while standing on the stage, but he originally did it while balancing on one foot, on a slack wire. Over the years Dieter tossed and caught as many as ten high while on the slack wire, and once he did a record stack of fourteen cups and saucers while standing on the ground during a rehearsal. Dieter said that It took him a full year to develop the confidence he needed to do the trick right every time. He said, "The 'Cups' turned out to be my big break. Before that I wasn't getting into the variety shows, but I started getting those jobs once I could do the Cups and Saucers, and doing it while balancing on the slack wire made me a unique circus act."

Getting back to 1977 and their viewing of Dieter at the Hacienda in Las Vegas: Tom Diehl said seeing his Hacienda act reconfirmed their belief he would be a great act for the *Bartlett Show*. Tom and Tommy talked with Dieter about coming to work for them, and Dieter said he was very interested, and a deal was made. Dieter was on stage at the *Bartlett Show* in Pigeon Forge, Tennessee, for the start of the 1978 season.

By this time Dieter was in his midforties and his body was telling him that someday he would have to eliminate the slack wire from his act, and maybe this was a good time. He was new to Tennessee and he felt it was probably the time to make that transition and discontinue using the slack wire. He stayed in Tennessee through the 1980 season, and then he went to the *Tommy Bartlett Show* at the Wisconsin Dells for the start of the 1981 season. He had talked with Tom and Tommy about dropping the slack wire and the evolution of his act as he aged. Tommy Bartlett had seen the reaction he was getting from the humorous patter Dieter was starting to incorporate into his act, and he said, "Dieter, you have the potential to be an unbelievably great comic. My suggestion is to continue to work more on your humorous patter, and your act will survive a lot longer than it would if you only juggle."

Dieter said that, originally the *Tommy Bartlett Show* was three performances a day, seven days a week, rain or shine. Then he told me about the time Tommy Bartlett flew Dieter to perform for a fundraising event in Chicago. Tommy Bartlett was a licensed pilot, and he had a long Chicago radio career. Tommy Bartlett and another Chicago radio personality, Irv Kupcinet, were best friends for many years. Every year Irv Kupcinet would put on a fund-raising event that was called Kup's Purple Heart Cruise on board a ship at Navy Pier. Each year Tommy would bring in acts for the event. One year it was Jim Grogan and the helicopter trapeze act. Another year it was Keith Abram who flew the big Delta Kite off one of the area skyscrapers, and so on. This year Tommy flew Dieter down to the old Meigs Field on the Chicago shoreline near Navy Pier where Dieter performed aboard the ship. He was a hit, and after the show they flew back to Wisconsin in time to do the 1:00 p.m. *Tommy Bartlett Show.* He added, "I did four shows in two states that day, one in Chicago and three at the Wisconsin Dells."

Speaking of flying planes, helicopters and kites, I want to mention a personal experience I had in 1984. At one point in the show, Eugene Nock, one of the legendary "Nerveless Nocks" flew a helicopter while Michael Nock did aerial stunts from a trapeze hanging from the bottom of the helicopter. Between shows Eugene would pilot a seaplane for a company that offered sightseeing tours of the Dells. On this particular day, Eugene asked me if I wanted to go along. He had one empty seat on his flight. While I had been a licensed pilot since 1962, I had never flown in a seaplane, and I jumped at the chance to go along for the ride. Later that summer Eugene Nock was again giving tours in the plane. After he landed, the other pilot took some other passengers up in the plane. Nobody yet knows why, but the Cessna 185A crashed shortly after takeoff and all on board died. Tom Diehl said he and Tommy happened to see it go down. Several of the *Bartlett Show* staff were swimming at the beach at the time, and the plane crashed within a few feet of where they were swimming.

Timeline #13, 1998 Tommy Bartlett: The Man, The Legend (Taken from TommyBartlett.com)

Tommy Bartlett is a household name. When you think Tommy Bartlett, you think skiing in Wisconsin Dells. Bartlett had an illustrious entertainment career spanning more than seventy years. His roots were in broadcasting. He started at age thirteen, working for WISN radio in his hometown of Milwaukee. He later moved on to television where, during a broadcast, he saw a water-ski show that became his inspiration.

The *Tommy Bartlett Water Ski & Jumping Boat Thrill Show* was born in 1952 as a traveling show out of Chicago. At only its second stop, Wisconsin Dells, the show was a hit, and local leaders asked Tommy and his crew to stay permanently. The *Wisconsin Dells Water Show* was born. Since then, what has evolved into the *Tommy Bartlett Show* has wowed audiences of all ages on the scenic shores of Lake Delton. The show's timeless appeal continues to make it one of the most favorite shows for families in Wisconsin Dells, enjoyed by generations.

Throughout the decades, the show continued to tour, performing at world's fairs and embarking on USO and other goodwill tours that exposed millions of people worldwide to the thrill of waterskiing. In the 1970s, Bartlett significantly expanded his show, which helped turn Wisconsin Dells into a major tourism destination. To this day, the *Tommy Bartlett Show* is a must-see Wisconsin Dells tourism event.

Throughout its history, Bartlett's water extravaganza has continually evolved, combining choreography, famous entertainers, amazing stunts, and state-of-the-art sound and visual technologies. It is the longest running, live, out-door entertainment show of its kind. Tommy Bartlett created good, wholesome family friendly entertainment. He brought it to the Dells and shared it with the world. More than twenty million spectators have experienced the vision of Tommy Bartlett at the Wisconsin Dells family show.

In 1993, after years of dedication to the sport, Bartlett, at age seventy-nine, was inducted into the Water Ski Hall of Fame in Cypress Gardens, Florida. Ironically, he only water-skied once in his life—on his seventieth birthday. Bartlett passed away in 1998. He was eighty-four.

Tommy Bartlett

Thomson "Tommy" Bartlett was a well-known Milwaukee (WISN) and Chicago (WBBM) radio personality and a born entertainer. During World War II he became a flight instructor for the United States Army Air Corps, and in 1947 he returned to radio, hosting a show called *Welcome, Travelers*. He is most likely best known for his *Tommy Bartlett Show*. Tommy was born in Milwaukee in 1914, and he died in Wisconsin Dells on September 6, 1998.

In 2007 Dieter's wife, Irene, became very ill. Dieter was now seventy-three years old and he reluctantly decided to retire after the

2007 season to care for Irene. And then, on June 9 of the 2008 season, the infamous Lake Delton disaster occurred. After several days of thunderstorms and tornadoes that dumped many inches of rain on Southern Wisconsin in a short period of time, Lake Delton's man-made embankment washed away, allowing the lake to drain into the Wisconsin River, taking several homes with it. Lake Delton was now empty. The *Bartlett Show*, as usual, was the source of summer employment for over a hundred college students, and the usual water show talent and crews were in place for the water show, but there was no lake. Local businesses that relied on the lake were also devastated. Several homes washed away and several others were destroyed. The disaster dominated the local and national news for days.

Both the show and the show's employees were sure to suffer. Tom Diehl said he couldn't just lay off all the water show employees, and he felt there was a possibility of keeping the show afloat without Lake Delton. In an effort that is still talked about in the Dells area, Tom Diehl's "The Show Must Go On" plan was soon underway. His first call was to Sarasota, to Dieter Tasso. He told Dieter what had happened. He said the lake was gone, and they needed to do the entire show as a stage show. The fate of everyone employed by the *Bartlett Show* was in trouble, because the entire show was in trouble. Tom asked Dieter if there was any chance he could help out. Dieter replied instantly. He said, "If Irene and I pack today, we could drive there in two days." That summer Wes Harrison came back, and several other acts were brought in to make it a full-length stage show. I attended several of the shows that summer. Tommy Bartlett always said, "We need to give the audience more than they are expecting. That summer the audiences had a rare experience…a great full-length show filled with variety acts from around the world.

Dieter has often said that he would gladly work anywhere where they needed a juggler, but for him, the *Tommy Bartlett Show* is home, and since the passing of his wife, Irene, in 2010, it's also a place of comfort and support.

The 2013 season would be his thirty-fifth year with the *Tommy Bartlett Show*. That kind of longevity in the entertainment field is extremely rare. Tom Diehl said, "As time went on, Dieter's routine evolved into a totally different routine than when we first brought him to the show." Diehl said, "He has been the most requested act we've ever had."

Timeline #14, 2010: Good Night, Irene

In April of 2010 Dieter shared with his friends, business acquaintances, and his fraternal family, the following account of the loss of, Irene, his loving wife of forty years.

"Good night, Irene, good night, Irene, I'll see you in my dreams." What a beautiful song! During the early seventies, the passengers of the Royal Caribbean cruise ship, the *Song of Norway*, were wondering why the captain of the ship was singing this song every evening over the public address system before his last announcement of the day. Only a few people knew that it was meant for my wife, Irene. Here is the story:

I am an entertainer. My name is Dieter Krakow (Dieter Tasso), and I was doing my Comedy Juggling Act, along with Irene on the *Song of Norway*. The captain liked my act, and he asked me if I would do a late show in a small cabaret room high in the ship. I was happy to do it, and every time I did it, I got a standing ovation. The reasons for that were that the captain stood up after every one of my performances. So the audience just had to do it too! Well, we got to be very good friends, and during one of our conversations he found out that Irene used to be an acrobat, and among other tricks could hang by her heels from the trapeze. He said, "Tomorrow, Irene, you will do this trick by the pool patio and I, the captain, will hang next to you by my toes."

Well they did it and the people went nuts. He was crazy about Irene from then on and sang to her every night.

We worked the ships for many years. Our work took us all over the world...with the Harlem Globetrotters to South America, Australia, and Europe. I can never forget when Irene entered the sports arena in Argentina in her short costume and blond hair to assist me in the act, the audience went screaming wild! She was a hot-looking mama! Nobody, but nobody paid any attention to my juggling anymore. However, I did not mind it at all; I was always happy and proud...of her and with her.

We spent over twenty years in Paris at the Crazy Horse Saloon. The trooper she was, she was always by my side. We worked Las Vegas, Wisconsin Dells, and shows with Bob Hope, Perry Como, Jimmy Dean, and many more. I never traveled alone; she was always with me, ever since we got married in June of 1970.

During the last couple of years we were not so lucky anymore. Irene started to get sick. It was pretty bad: twice cancer, twice a heart attack, and then a stroke. We had to stay home in Sarasota, close to her doctors. The stroke happened on January 31, 2010. A blood vessel broke in her head around 5:00 p.m. When I helped her to bed, I knew she could not lift her left arm anymore. She was paralyzed. I called 911, and she fell into a coma within minutes. At the hospital the CT scan showed that her skull was full of blood and our doctor told me that "there was no hope." For five hours I held her hand. I did not want her to die, but I knew she would. I don't know, but I hoped she knew I was there.

I kept watching the monitor and the beating of her heart until around 10:00 p.m., when she finally closed her beautiful eyes forever. "It happened so very fast!" Well, that is actually what she always wanted. Still, I am so very grateful for the forty wonderful and happy years we had together. She was one in a million, and I will always love her! So..."Good night, Irene, good night, Irene, I'll see you in my dreams."

Dieter and Irene Krakow

Timeline #15, And the Beat Goes On

In the off-season Dieter continues to perform at the wonderful GOP Variety Theatres as well as the various other venues. In Germany he is loved by the crowds that fill the house for the show.

A Streetcar in Düsseldorf Germany advertising the Apollo Variety Theatre

Each year, for many years, Dieter has entertained at various venues in Germany including the magnificent Wintergarten, which has a great tradition, dating back to 1887 when the original Wintergarten variety theatre wowed audiences in Berlin. It ended during World War II, and then in 2010 it was reopened. The new Wintergarten premiered with the *Great Variety Show*, which paid homage to the old Wintergarten's illustrious past.

Since then, three lavish, in-house variety shows have been playing for audiences all year round, and the theatre has also rebooted the classic dining theatre concept with a contemporary *Show and Dine* that is known for its style and class.

Wintergarten Variety Theatre, Twenty-Year Anniversary Show, Berlin (September 25, 2012)

Bookings closer to home included doing family shows January through April at Busch Gardens, which is a short commuting distance from his home. "Home every night, and a day off every week around the house... It is great!"

Uncle Otto and Aunt Klara's son, Sascha, were Dieter's only relative here in the United States. Dieter and Sascha are very close. Sascha was born in 1949. He is the controller for one of the grand beachfront hotels on the ocean in East Sarasota, but Dieter stressed that Sascha was also an extremely talented juggler. Several times Dieter included Sascha in his act and he was always an enormous hit. Dieter said, "It came naturally to him. He had a great personality and was always a big hit with the audience, but Aunt Klara, didn't want him to get into show business."

Dieter's parents died in the 1940s during the war. Uncle Otto and Aunt Klara have also both passed. Uncle Otto died in 1959, while Dieter was entertaining in North Africa. Aunt Klara died in 1994, in the United States. Dieter's older brother lived in Belgium and has also died. Dieter's sisters, Dorathea "Thea" and Christa, still live in Germany. He visits them on his bookings in Germany. Regarding his sister, Thea, Dieter chuckled and said, "She's a lively, loveable ninety-two-year-old chatty Berliner. He jokingly said, "She speaks one hundred forty words a minute with gusts up to one hundred eighty."

Between bookings and in the off-season Dieter lives in Sarasota, Florida. Like Dieter, many of his Sarasota friends come from families with generations as circus performers. Some families go back several hundred years in the circus. They grew up in that world. Sarasota is also the home of Circus Sarasota and Sailor Circus. Sailor Circus is a circus school. The area is also the home of much circus history. Dieter is active with Show Folks of Sarasota, which is a social group. I would love to sit in on some of their get-togethers and listen to the stories that are told.

I once asked Dieter how well he knew the late Karl Wallenda. He said, "Well, I bought my first lot in Sarasota from Karl Wallenda. The lot was only a hundred feet by a hundred feet." Then he added, "It wasn't very wide or deep. Karl sold me by stressing the height."

Timeline #16, Epilogue

I have had an extremely enjoyable time doing a series of telephone interviews with Dieter, collecting the stories for this book. I was intrigued from start to finish. At one point Dieter told me that he would like to somehow personally thank each individual person who cared enough to read the story of his life. What follows is not to "all" those who read the book; it is more personal. It is to "each" person who has read this book. Dieter said:

I am grateful to have been able to live my life as an entertainer, to have traveled to so many exciting places in the world, and to have met so many wonderful people. I have made many friends along the way. I have to admit that I've had quite an exciting life so far, and I probably would have enough stories for a second book, with all that I have forgotten to mention.

Then again, the highway of my life was not always the smoothest. There were quite a few bumps along the way and there were times which were not easy to live through, but all in all, I am *very grateful* for it all, and I am especially grateful to the millions of people I had the pleasure to perform for over the years. Your wonderful laughter and your applause made the good times great and the bad times endurable. To all of you, *my dear audience*, and to those who cared enough to read about my life in this book, I sincerely offer a heartfelt *thank you!*

Timeline #17, An At-a-Glance and Summary

1947–1952   Working Berlin and comes to America

1952   Madison Square Garden, Boston Garden, Ringling Brothers
Cuba Fulgencio Batista in audience

1953   The Ed Sullivan TV Show, May 3, with Joe Louis & Barbara
Stanwyck

1954   Ringling Bros. and Barnum & Bailey

1955   Blinstrub's through agent Al Dobritch

1956   The Ed Sullivan TV Show, March 4, with Gary Cooper &
Burt Lancaster
The Patti Page TV Show, July 7, with Johnny Puleo &
Harmonica Rascals and Julius LaRosa

1957   The Jackie Gleason All Star Circus Review on March 5 with
Emmett Kelly & Hugh O'Brian
The Toronto Sports Show
The Gene Autry Show. Traveled to gigs with Gene on his
twin-engine D-18 Beechcraft.
The Gleason Buffalo Shows (with The Wallendas)
The Clyde Brothers Circus in Syracuse
The Hamilton Standard Circus, Hartford Connecticut
(thirteen years after the horrible tent fire)
The Fort Worth Shrine Circus

1958   The Ed Sullivan TV Show, August 10, with Sam Levenson
The Tom Packs Circus
The New Orleans Shrine Circus
The St. Louis Shrine Circus
The Omaha Shrine Circus
The Minneapolis Auto Show (Sport Show with Pat Boone
The Cristiani Brothers Circus
The Atlanta Shrine Circus

1959   The Circus Scott in Sweden, all the way up in Kiruna
Algiers & Oran in N. Africa. The revolution killed up to one
and a half million people over ten years

1960–1963   The Cristiani Brothers Circus
The Alhambra Temple Shrine Circus
The Harold Brothers Circus

1964   The Ed Sullivan TV Show January 5 with Count Basie and
Jane Powell

1967   The Harlem Globetrotters, seven years

1968   Blinstrub's "Blinnie's" (the Blinstrub fire was in 1968)

1968   The Merv Griffin TV Show, Oct. 8, with Don DeFore and
Jack Carter

1969   The Merv Griffin TV Show, Dec. 9, with Diane Keaton &
Barbara McNair

1970 - 1976   Cruise Ships

1970–1990   Crazy Horse in Paris France

1977   The Garden Bros. Circus
Circus Vargas
St. Croix, Virgin Islands

1978   The new Chuck Barris Rah-Rah-Show, March 7, on NBC-T V

1978–1980   Pigeon Forge, Tennessee, the *Tommy Bartlett Show*

1981–To the present The *Tommy Bartlett Show*, Memorial Day through Labor Day, GOP Variety Shows, and Wintergarten Variety Shows in Germany off-season and family shows January through April at Busch Gardens

Other books by Ron Dentinger

Dear Ron is like "Dear Abby" but funny. For twenty years Ron wrote a humor column for the *Dodgeville Chronicle,* and for twenty years there would be those occasional fictitious letters from fictitious readers asking for advice. It was always interesting as to what was stupider, the questions or the replies.

How to Argue with Your Spouse is written in collaboration with Rich Renik and Chuck Gekus. The book is a short, tongue-in-cheek, tabletop-type gender-neutral, pseudo-marriage-manual originally published through Kendall-Hunt in 1996. It is now available again from Amazon.com.

Down Time is a joke book that includes a short section about using humor in a banquet setting. There is also a short section dealing with: "How to Write Your Own Jokes." Down Time was published in 1994 by Kendall-Hunt. It is out of print, but used copies are quite often available through Amazon.com.

Contact: e-mail: laughter@mhtc.net, Phone: 608-574-6924